D1101260

[UNDERSTANDING GRAMMAR]

PHRASES, CLAUSES *and*
CONJUNCTIONS

A N N   R I G G S

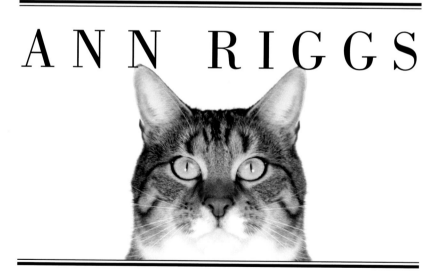

W
FRANKLIN WATTS
LONDON • SYDNEY

First published in the UK in 2012 by
Franklin Watts
338 Euston Road
London NW1 3BH

Franklin Watts Australia
Level 17/207 Kent Street
Sydney, NSW 2000

First published by Creative Education, an imprint of The Creative Company.

Copyright © 2012 Creative Education.

A CIP catalogue record for this book is available from the British Library.

ISBN: 978 1 4451 1077 6

Dewey number: 425.7

Printed in China

Franklin Watts is a division of
Hachette Children's Books,
an Hachette UK company.

www.hachette.co.uk

Design and production by Liddy Walseth
Art direction by Rita Marshall
Photographs by Corbis (Hulton-Deutsch Collection), Getty Images
(Archive Photos, Anne Frank Fonds-Basel/Anne Frank House-Amsterdam, Michael Blann,
Tobi Corney, Kim Sayer, Kim Taylor, Tom and Steve), iStockphoto
(Jill Battaglia, Andrea Gingerich, Eileen Hart, Hypergon, Eric Isselée, Guillermo Lobo,
Chris Price, Steve Snowden, Srdjan Srdjanov, Syagci, James Trice)
page 35: Paul Risdale Pictures/Alamy

TABLE of CONTENTS

Music swells. Siblings squabble. Owls hoot. I am. Grammar is. As simply as that,

two words can become a SENTENCE. The information in a short sentence can

be expanded by adding more words that give vivid descriptions or specific

reactions. Where should the words be placed? How does a writer know what

PUNCTUATION to use? And what does all of this mean? Words fall into place

more easily when one has an understanding of grammar, a system of rules

that gives writers the foundation for producing acceptable formal expression.

It is this acceptable form, this appropriate grammar, that helps readers

comprehend what has been written.

Basic sentences have a subject (someone or something) and a PREDICATE or verb

(action or state of being). Within sentences are groups of words called phrases and

clauses. A phrase is a group of related words without subject and verb that acts like

one PART OF SPEECH, such as the phrase 'in the meantime' (which acts like an adverb,

or a word that describes a verb) or the expression 'lose your bottle' (phrasal verb) or

the description 'hovering in the branches' (adjective). How are the words related?

Although each word is still its own part of speech the group functions as a unit.

Clauses are different from phrases in that they have a subject and a verb. A sentence may have one clause or several but the minimum requirement is one, as all clauses – and all sentences – need to have at least one group of words with a subject and a verb. When a clause can stand by itself and make sense it's called independent. When it cannot exist on its own it's called dependent, and often needs the help of a connecting word, a conjunction, to attach it to a MAIN CLAUSE. Conjunctions can co-ordinate, SUBORDINATE and CORRELATE but, whatever they do, they always make phrases and clauses communicate within and between sentences. Without all three parts – phrases, additional clauses and conjunctions – our sentences would all have the same stark structure: one clause of one subject and one verb. Adding other words gives writers a way to increase variety in their work and bring sentences to life!

FLAWLESS PHRASES

One of the most common types of phrases is the prepositional phrase. In it, a preposition with its noun or pronoun OBJECT relates to another word in the sentence, as in this example with the common prepositions *from* and *for*: **This is *from* me *for* you.** The rules of grammar state that a preposition should appear just next to its object (as with the previous objects, 'me' and 'you') and that a sentence should never end with a preposition. But sometimes it is acceptable to bend the rules in order to make the sentence sound more like natural speech.

PREPOSITIONS

about	above	across	after	against
along	amidst	amongst	around	as
at	before	behind	below	beneath
beside	besides	between	beyond	but (meaning except)
by	concerning	considering	despite	down
during	except	excepting	excluding	for
from	in	in front of	inside	into
like	near	of	off	on
onto	opposite	outside	over	past
per	regarding	since	than	through
throughout	to	together with	toward	towards
under	underneath	unlike	until	up
upon	via	with	within	without

TABLE 1

Here's an example: **She's not the person I talked *with*.** Although we're ending a sentence with a preposition, it is less formal and easier to understand than this: **She's not the person *with* whom I talked.** Similarly, saying **Where did that come *from*?** instead of ***From* where did that come?** fits better into a conversation. It is never permissible, however, to end a sentence with an unnecessary preposition: **Where is he *at*?** or **Where did she go *to*?** Before we go on, see Table 1 above for a review of commonly used prepositions.

Prepositional phrases have many functions within sentences but their most important job is building relationships between words. One way to identify a prepositional phrase is to find the sentence's subject and verb, and then see what's left. In *The Indian in the Cupboard* (1980) by British author Lynne Banks (1929–), Omri, the main character, encounters (and attempts to conceal from his family) toys that come alive. Find the 15 prepositional phrases in the short excerpt on the following page.

" Breakfast in his house was often a dicey meal anyway, with everybody more or less bad-tempered... Under cover of the moans that went up about the prospect of no apples in the autumn, and the exclamations about the size of the hailstones, Omri slipped his coat on and ran through the bouncing ice lumps to school. On the way he stopped under a protecting yew tree and took the little men out. He showed them each a large hailstone, which, to them, was the size of a football. "

The main parts of these sentences are:

> Breakfast was often a dicey meal anyway. Omri slipped his coat on and ran. He stopped and took the little men out. He showed them each a large hailstone, which was the size.

The last part doesn't make much sense without the ending prepositional phrase '*of* a football', does it? We have found the action but all the details and relationships are missing! In the first sentence, '*in* his house' modifies, or describes, 'breakfast', while '*with* everybody more or less bad-tempered' tells more about the noun 'meal'. When '*Under* cover' tells us how Omri got out of his house, '*of* the moans... and the exclamations' describes what kind of 'cover' he had. The three phrases '*about* the prospect', '*of* no apples' and '*in* the autumn' tell more about each other and give more information about the sentence as a whole. Similarly, the next phrases in line are integral to understanding the entire sentence: Without '*of* the hailstones', the description '*about* the size' doesn't make sense. And if we take out both phrases, we have no clue why anyone is exclaiming at all. The sentence ends by describing where Omri ran: '*through* the bouncing ice lumps' and '*to* school'. In the next sentence, we know when and where Omri stopped: '*On* the way' and '*under* a protecting yew tree'. Finally, the last sentence ends with '*to* them', an object phrase, and '*of* a football', a descriptive phrase about the hailstone. Who knew prepositions and their objects could relate to other words in so many different ways!

Prepositional phrases make up only one kind of word group. Three types of verb forms called verbals can also make phrases. Verbals may look like verbs but they can never function as the main verb of a sentence. A gerund is a verbal noun and can be used

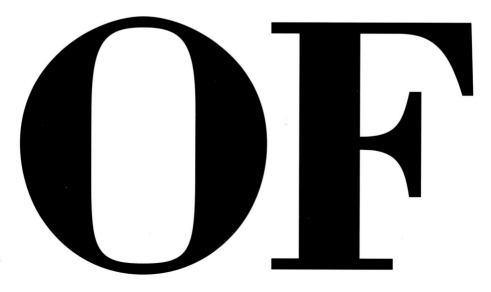

in a sentence in all the ways a noun can. In the sentence, **I appreciate his *keeping me informed***, *keeping* is a gerund; '*keeping me informed*' is a gerund phrase, the direct object (a noun phrase that receives the action of a verb) of the verb 'appreciate'. Also of note in this example is the correct use of the possessive pronoun 'his' before the gerund, showing ownership of the verbal, rather than the OBJECTIVE CASE, as in **I appreciate *him* keeping me informed.** The second type of verbal is the participle, which can also be used as an adjective. Notice the adjective phrase in this sentence: **The estate agent *receiving the most referrals* will be rewarded.** The participle *receiving* is in the present TENSE and '*receiving* the most referrals' is the participial phrase modifying 'estate agent'. The third verbal, an infinitive, is defined as '*to* and a verb'. Infinitives can function as nouns or as modifiers. In the next example, the infinitive phrase is the subject of the sentence: ***To be prepared* for anything is a lofty ambition.** However, in **Abby felt an irresistible urge *to exercise***, the infinitive *to exercise* acts as an adjective, describing the noun 'urge'.

See if you can spot 10 prepositional phrases and 5 infinitives in the last paragraph from US president Abraham Lincoln's (1809–65) second INAUGURAL ADDRESS of 4 March 1865. Refer to the listing of prepositions in Table 1 if you need to and remember, '*to* and a verb' makes an infinitive.

TO+VERB

" With malice toward none; with charity for all; with firmness in the right, as God gives us to see the right, let us strive on to finish the work we are in; to bind up the nation's wounds; to care for him who shall have borne the battle, and for his widow and his orphan – to do all which may achieve and cherish a just and lasting peace among ourselves, and with all nations. "

ABRAHAM LINCOLN,

REPUBLICAN CANDIDATE FOR PRESIDENT OF THE UNITED STATES.

The first four words make up two prepositional phrases; together they describe how to 'strive on'. Similarly, '*with* charity' and '*for* all' are also coupled as one adverb, as are '*with* firmness' and '*in* the right'. Phrases seven ('*for* him') and eight ('*for* his widow and his orphan') complete the 'to care' infinitive phrase as nouns and a pronoun used as COMPOUND OBJECTS, while the last two ('*among* ourselves' and '*with* all nations') are used as adjectives that modify the noun 'peace'. Did you notice that the infinitive phrases also had prepositions with nouns or pronouns after them? Have another look at Lincoln's goals for the unified nation.

If we removed all the prepositional and infinitive phrases, the result would be 'as God gives us, let us strive on, and'. This isn't much to go on, is it? While it may not have been Lincoln's intent, he has given us an impressive grammar lesson in the importance of prepositional and infinitive phrases.

FOR HIS WIDOW &HIS ORPHAN

Verbs – but not verbs

Fill in each underlined word with an alternative verb that ends in *-ing*:

SWIMMING IS GOOD EXERCISE.
SHARON ENJOYS TYPING AT WORK.
MARK'S FAVOURITE PASTIME IS READING.

Your choices of a subject, a direct object and a predicate nominative (a noun in the predicate that renames the subject) were all used as nouns – they were gerunds. This time write each of those *-ing* words in your own sentences, using them to describe someone

or something. Your *-ing* verbs will now function as adjectives – they'll become participles. Finally, write three more sentences that correctly use infinitives ('*to* and a verb') as nouns or modifiers, such as this direct object: 'Does the car need *to be washed*?'

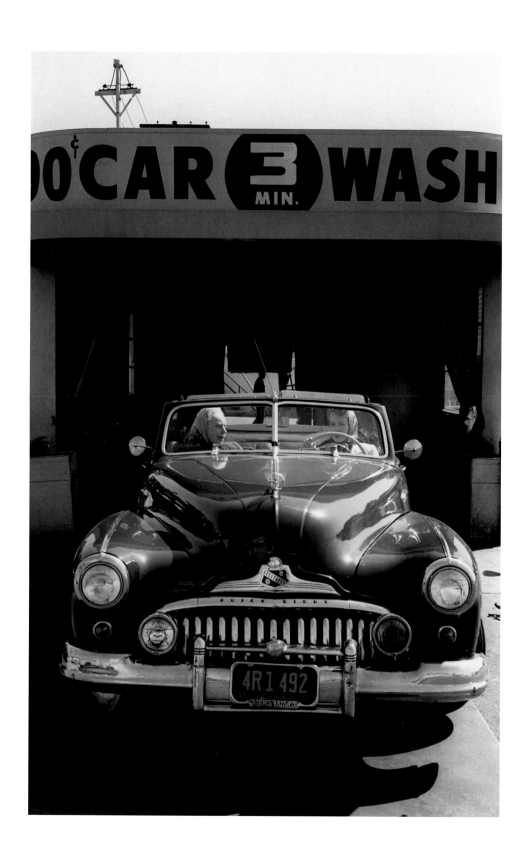

FURTHER PHRASAL DIVERSITY

Other types of phrases connect certain components of a sentence to add meaning. Transitional phrases assist the writer in organising thoughts, helping ideas flow smoothly from the first point to the last. They often begin with a preposition or an adverb. See Table 2 for some of the most common transitions.

During the Second World War (1939–45), a Jewish girl living in the Netherlands received a diary for her 13th birthday. This became Anne Frank's amazing story of the two years she and her family were in hiding before being captured by the police of Nazi Germany, the Gestapo. Find Anne's transition that contrasts one way of thinking with another in the following excerpt dated 7 March 1944.

TRANSITIONAL PHRASES

after all	as a result	at any rate
at the same time	by the way	even so
for example	in addition	in conclusion
in contrast	in fact	in other words
in the first place	on the contrary	on the other hand

TABLE 2

" I don't see how Mummy's idea can be right, because then how are you supposed to behave if you go through the misery yourself? Then you are lost. On the contrary, I've found that there is always some beauty left – in nature, sunshine, freedom, in yourself; these can all help you... And whoever is happy will make others happy too. He who has courage and faith will never perish in misery! **"**

A photo of Anne Frank aged 13 in 1942

Do you hear the diarist's emphatic voice? After analysing her mother's view, stating how she opposes it, Anne uses the transitional phrase 'on the contrary'. Using the transition as she does, the reader is watching for a contrasting view. Although Anne wasn't writing her diary for others to read, the form makes it easy to follow and the relationship between the ideas is clear because of it.

Another phrase type, a PARTICIPIAL PREPOSITIONAL PHRASE, may seem like a contradiction in terms. While a participle is a verb form that can show action or modify a noun, it can also sometimes function as a preposition with an object: *Considering the lateness* **of the hour, the chairman shortened the business meeting.** In this way, a participial preposition can be substituted for a phrasal preposition, or two or more words used as one preposition. Instead of the phrase 'with regard to', say 'regarding' if you're talking about something like 'the last item on the agenda'.

The next phrase category is the familiar verb phrase. In this phrase, a main verb and a HELPING VERB are used as a unit, such as: **Ella *has broken* her wrist again; I *have looked* everywhere for that book; The package** *should have been delivered* **yesterday.** Writers need to pay particular attention to verb phrases to be sure they agree with subjects, matching singular helping verbs with singular subjects and plural helping verbs with plural subjects. And when *or* connects the parts of a COMPOUND SUBJECT, the subject closer to the verb determines the choice of the helper. The following example uses plural subject *buses* and plural verb *are*: **Either the early bus or the later *buses are* meant to take all the equipment.** In the next sentence, however, the singular subject *sponsor* is nearer to the singular verb *is*: **The parents or the *sponsor is* going to sign the forms.** Verb phrases separated by an adverb modifier such as *not* may be trickier to identify, as in **They *have not heard* the end of this.** Just remember to find the action verb (*heard*) and then look for the helping verb (*have*).

As we've seen, there are many kinds of phrases but each is a group of two or more words used for one purpose. Sometimes the phrase even acts as one word. A phrasal adjective, also known as a compound modifier, describes a noun and is often hyphenated:

WITH EMPHATIC VOICE!

A *state-inspected* school has high standards; The *lower-than-average* earnings surprised no one; and The black-and-white film won many awards. Another phrase category, the phrasal adverb, has two or more words but it functions as one adverb. Adverbs modify verbs, adjectives and other adverbs by answering the questions of *how?*, *when?*, *where?*, *why?* and *how much?*, as in the following examples: As a *result* of the vote, the measure failed (*why*); Dog toys were found *here and there* throughout the house (*where*). A compound adverb, while appearing as a single word, can be divided into at least two smaller words used together as one adverb: *other + wise* is *otherwise*; *further + more* is *furthermore*; and *not + with + standing* is *notwithstanding*.

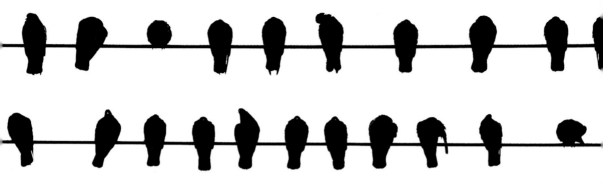

Finally, there is the phrasal verb, a group of words not defined by their original meanings. This category has a separate purpose – it's not meant to be taken LITERALLY. Phrasal verbs can be made up of a verb and a preposition or adverb – or they can be made up of a preposition and an adverb – plus one or more nouns or pronouns. Here are some common expressions using phrasal verbs: to **back up** the hard drive, someone you can **count on**, going to **keep tabs on** you. Backing up the computer's hard drive (making another copy of the files) certainly doesn't mean you do that while walking backwards. And having a trusted friend has nothing to do with a maths equation, unless you're studying together. While an interest in keeping track of someone's activities may be important, attaching actual tags to the person is not necessary.

Phrasal verbs are used in conversation and informal writing and this is the key to our understanding them. As we want to write acceptable, well-constructed sentences, we need to know what to avoid as well as what is appropriate. When a person has been told to **get over it** rather than 'to try to resolve his feelings', the message is an IDIOM. Idiomatic phrasal verbs may also reflect certain dialects, or regional speech patterns. If someone says he's ready to **hang up his boots,** he's ready to retire from sport, not just put away his gear. Anybody who is told **The ball is in your court now** would need to understand that it's up to her to make a decision. And when a person wants to express a different opinion, perhaps putting himself in a tough position, he may begin by saying **I'm going to go out on a limb here.** No gymnasium is in sight, no trees worthy of climbing are nearby but the phrasal verbs make their unique meanings known. Such idioms are especially challenging to students learning English as a second language. In fact, the grammatical classification of phrasal verbs is often lost on native speakers as well! A dictionary is the best tool for learning phrasal verbs. Try looking up a main verb such as 'get' and see how many phrasal verb entries you can find. Remember that generally idioms are not to be used in formal expression, such as school assignments.

Say this instead

Idioms (page 21) are not to be used in formal expression, such as for essays or other school homework. This is an exercise in ensuring you know what not to say! Listed below

1. SPILL THE BEANS
2. ARGUE THE TOSS
3. CLEAN UP YOUR ACT
4. BITE OFF MORE THAN YOU CAN CHEW
5. BURST YOUR BUBBLE

are phrasal verbs that are not meant to be taken literally. Work out what each idiom means and use the definition in a sentence of your own. Dictionary entries for each verb (the first word) of the expression will point to phrase usages as well.

6. LOSE YOUR BOTTLE
7. SCRATCH THE SURFACE
8. CALL IT A DAY
9. BURN YOUR BRIDGES
10. FLOG A DEAD HORSE

FORMING ALLIANCES

As well as independent clauses, there are dependent (or subordinate) clauses. Words called conjunctions have different functions according to the types of clauses they join. Co-ordinating conjunctions (*and*, *or*, *but*, *for*, *nor*, *yet* and *so*), the strongest of the connecting words, join independent clauses in sentences, other clauses and words within clauses. A COMPOUND SENTENCE has two independent clauses connected with a co-ordinating conjunction, such as **Jan's family invited Beth to go with them on holiday *but* she couldn't find anyone to work her shift that week.** Beginning a sentence with a co-ordinating conjunction is a way to add variety of expression. *And* it is permissible when the two sentences are closely related.

When a dependent clause needs help to connect to a main clause, we use a subordinating conjunction: ***If* the telephone rings, don't answer it. Keep practising *until* you can play the piece for your music teacher. Sid wants us to pick him up *because* his mum doesn't have a car this week.** As the previous example sentences show, clues for recognising dependent clauses come from the words that introduce them. Table 3 on the opposite page is a helpful source for dependent clause clue words.

The conjunction *than* demands special attention when it begins a dependent clause in a sentence such as this one: **Stuart is taller *than* I.** You might be tempted to say, **Stuart is taller *than* me** but you'd be wrong.

SUBORDINATING CONJUNCTIONS

after	although	as far as/ soon as	as if/even if	because
before	how	now/now that	once	since
than	that/so that	then	though/as though	until
when/ whenever	where/ wherever	whether	while	why

TABLE 3

THAT

Why? One part of that sentence can stand alone: **Stuart is taller.** But the subordinating conjunction *than* means the sentence has both an independent and a dependent clause. The tricky part is that the dependent part of the sentence is an incomplete comparison – it isn't all there. In our example, 'than I' really

a complete thought. Many dependent clauses function in the sentence as adverbs that modify verbs, adjectives or other adverbs. *That*, *which* and *where* can begin clauses of more than one kind, however, and may be adjectives or adverbs depending on the purpose of the clause in the sentence.

WHICH

means 'than I am'. Adding 'am' clarifies the relationship of the verb with its subject pronoun 'I'. The object pronoun 'me' has no place in the comparison.

The subordinate clause is a sentence FRAGMENT if left unconnected to an independent clause, so always join the dependent and independent clauses to make

Keeping the word clues in mind, see if you can work out what the following sentences have in common:

(1) If I only had an hour to chop down a tree, I would spend the first 45 minutes sharpening my axe.

(2) My father taught me to work; he did not teach me to love it.

WHERE

Firstly, US president Abraham Lincoln, known for his hard work, is given credit for having said both. Secondly, in each of the complete sentences there is also an independent clause. Thirdly, between the beginning capital letter and the full stop in each sentence are two groups of words with a subject and verb. For our purposes, this is where the similarities end. Considering the first sentence as a whole, *if* is a clue that the words before the comma are dependent upon the main clause for support. Even with its subject (*I*), verb (*had*), direct object (*hour*), infinitive (*to chop*) and prepositional phrase (*down* a tree), the beginning *if* makes the clause subordinate – dependent. The comma after 'tree' shows where that subordinate clause ends. What 'I' (Lincoln – subject) 'would spend' (verb) 45 minutes doing is the part of the sentence that can stand alone; it's the independent clause.

Sentence two has a different punctuation clue; this time it's a semicolon that ends the first independent clause and shows where the second one begins. Both parts of the second sentence are independent and can make sense on their own: in the first part, the subject is 'father' and the verb is 'taught'; in the second part, the subject is 'he' and the verb is 'did... teach'. Because they are related by Lincoln having mentioned his father and the subject of work, both independent clauses can be in the same compound sentence.

Relative clauses are dependent. They're called relative because they relate, or establish ties, to the independent, main clause of the sentence. The first word of a relative clause is a relative pronoun (*that, what, which, who, whoever, whom, whose*). The relative clause may be used as a subject, a direct object, an object of a preposition, or an appositive (a word that follows a noun, renaming and supplying more information about it). In **The puppy *that* Cheryl chased didn't have a collar,** the subordinate clause '*that* Cheryl chased' is used as an appositive and gives more information about the subject noun, 'puppy'. It is possible to be more concise and omit the relative pronoun *that* as the meaning of the sentence is clearly understood; this is known as an elliptical (meaning something has been left out) construction: **The puppy Cheryl chased didn't have a collar.** The important thing to remember is to relate the main clause to the subordinate clause and that this is often done with a relative pronoun.

A healthy perspective

According to Richard Carlson (1961–2006), American author of *Don't Sweat the Small Stuff for Teens* (2000), thinking more about what's right with your life than what's wrong with it can be a helpful and healthy habit to form. In the previous sentence, the subordinating conjunction *than* was a clue for a dependent clause. Try integrating some subordinating conjunctions into your own writing. Using at least five words from Table 3 on page 25 to tie the clauses in your sentences together, write about a positive person whom you know and how his or her outlook has affected you. Why is this person's optimism a trait you would want to pass on to others?

RELATING, CORRELATING AND CO-OPERATING

T o practise spotting dependent clauses read the following excerpt from 'Beware of the Dog' (1944), a short story about a Second World War bomber pilot by British author Roald Dahl (1916–90). After ejecting from his plane, the pilot wakes up in hospital – which he is told is in his home country of England. However, he soon begins to suspect that he is actually in enemy territory. Can you identify all the dependent clauses? Don't forget about relative clause clue words!

" Slowly the grain of doubt grew, and with it came fear, a light,
dancing fear that warmed but did not frighten; the kind of
fear that one gets not because one is afraid, but because one feels that there
is something wrong. Quickly the doubt and the fear grew so that he became
restless and angry, and when he touched his forehead with his hand he found it
was damp with sweat. He knew then that he must do something; that he must
find some way of proving to himself that he was either right or wrong, and he
looked up and saw again the window and the green curtains... Somehow he
must reach it and look out... But what about his leg? He put his hand underneath
the bedclothes and felt the thick bandaged stump which was all that was left on
the right-hand side. It seemed all right. It didn't hurt. But it would not be easy.

"

Roald Dahl, shown in 1971

IF THEN ALL

Of the five dependent clauses in sentence one, the first two *that* clauses are adjectives – one modifies the noun 'fear' and the other describes the noun 'kind'. The two *because* clauses are adverbs qualifying the verb 'gets'. The last *that* clause, **that there is something wrong,** is used as an adverb telling how one 'feels' and it completes the thought.

In the second sentence, **that he became restless and angry** and **when he touched his forehead with his hand** are both adverb clauses, the first modifying the verb 'grew', the second qualifying the verb 'found'. Did you also notice the elliptical construction in that sentence? The clause (**that**) **it was damp with sweat** is the answer to what he found and serves as the direct object. The third sentence has more noun clauses and objects: **that he must do something** and **that he must find some way of proving to himself** explain what he knew, while **that he was either right or wrong** is the object of the gerund (the verbal noun that is used as the object of the preposition *of*) 'proving'. Our last dependent clauses in the excerpt describe the pilot's amputated leg, one noun appositive referring to the stump (**which was all**) and another (**that was left on the right-hand side**) that renames the predicate noun 'all'. Without the subordinate clauses, we can get the gist of the story but there are obvious holes:

Slowly the grain of doubt grew, and with it came fear, a light, dancing fear _ _ _ _ _ _; the kind of fear _ _ _ not _ _ _ _, but _ _ _ _ _ _ _. Quickly the doubt and the fear grew so _ _ _ _ _ _, and _ _ _ _ _ _ _ _ he found _ _ _ _ _. He knew then _ _ _ _ _; _ _ _ _ _ _ _ _ _ _ _ _ _ _ _ _, and he looked up and saw again the window and the green curtains.

CORRELATIVE CONJUNCTIONS

as–as	both–and	either–or
if–then	neither–nor	not only–but also
so–as	where–there	whether–or

TABLE 4

Notice how unemotional those first three sentences are without the dependent clauses. We're missing the pilot's very thoughts and feelings that drive him towards restlessness and give him clues that something is very wrong. The true meaning of those sentences depends upon the clauses that relate descriptive information to the parts that remain.

When words, phrases and clauses correlate, they work together in a comparable, shared relationship. Correlative conjunctions are used in pairs to show the connection between the ideas expressed in different parts of the same sentence, to join consecutive clauses that depend on each other to make one complete thought. The parts of the sentence they correlate must be parallel – structurally alike – using, for example, infinitive phrases, verbs or clauses with each half of the pair, as in these examples: **The assignment was *not only* to read the book *but also* to watch the film. Claudia was *both* praised by her manager *and* admired by her secretary. *If* the rule cannot be changed, *then* everyone must abide by it.** Table 4 shows the correlative conjunction pairs most frequently used.

Sometimes adverbs function as conjunctions in sentences as well. When that happens a conjunctive adverb either joins two independent clauses (with the help of a semicolon) or it joins a dependent to an independent clause. The dependent clause that follows the conjunctive adverb will answer how, when, where, why or how much: **Floodwaters covered the motorway; *consequently*, we had to take a diversion.** Why did we have to take a diversion? The dependent clause following the adverb *consequently* refers the reader to the

main clause and the floodwaters. **Stella sat waiting for her dad to collect her; *meanwhile*, her friends went to the shops.** When did Stella's friends go to the shops? This adverb clause points to the information in the main clause about Stella having to wait for her dad. Do you see the punctuation clue for the end of the independent clause? There is a semicolon before the conjunctive adverb and a comma after it. See Table 5 for examples of adverbs used as conjunctions to begin dependent clauses.

CONJUNCTIVE ADVERBS

again	also	although	besides	consequently
finally	furthermore	hence	however	incidentally
indeed	instead	likewise	meanwhile	moreover
naturally	nevertheless	next	nonetheless	otherwise
similarly	still	then	therefore	thus

TABLE 5

BUILD YOUR OWN SENTENCE

Friend or foe?

Find and read the entire story of Roald Dahl's injured airman, 'Beware of the Dog'. Choose the viewpoint of the British pilot or of the hospital nurse and write a letter to your family describing the attempted deception. How do you feel about what is going on – about the injury, the recovery and the other people involved? Work out a way to use at least three sets of correlative conjunctions, such as *if–then*, from Table 4 on page 33 to explain how you are affected by the circumstances. Also use at least three conjunctive adverbs (Table 5, page 34) as you describe the *how, when, where, why* or *how much* about your situation.

KNOWING ALL THE ANGLES

To see how a writer can benefit from an understanding of the various kinds of phrases, clauses and conjunctions, look at this excerpt from *Gifted Hands: The Ben Carson Story* (1990) by surgeon Ben Carson (1951–). As you read the compelling information given in this non-fiction account of a young girl's struggle with seizures, take notice of the clue words for prepositional phrases, dependent clauses and conjunctions. Try to identify the conjunctive adverb (page 34) in the first sentence.

"Although born normal, Maranda Francisco had her first grand mal seizure at 18 months, a convulsion characteristic of epilepsy that we sometimes call an electrical storm in the brain. Two weeks later Maranda suffered a second grand mal seizure, and her doctor put her on anti-convulsive medication.

By her fourth birthday, the seizures were becoming more frequent. They also changed, suddenly affecting only the right side of her body. She didn't lose consciousness; the seizures were focal (half a grand mal), originating in the left side of her brain and disrupting only the right side of her body. Each seizure left Maranda weak on her right side, sometimes unable to talk normally for as long as two hours. By the time I heard about her situation, Maranda was experiencing up to 100 seizures a day, as often as three minutes apart, making the right side of her body useless... Only during sleep was she seizure-free...

Maranda manages well without the left half of her brain because of a phenomenon we call plasticity. We know that the two halves of the brain aren't as rigidly divided as we once thought. Although both have distinct functions, one side has the major responsibility for language and the other for artistic ability. But children's brains have a considerable overlap. In plasticity, functions once governed by a set of cells in the brain are taken over by another set of cells. No one understands exactly how this works."

A conjunctive adverb phrase – *Although born normal* – leads into the main clause of sentence one, which features a prepositional phrase that tells when Maranda's first seizure occurred. In the dependent *that* clause of sentence one, another prepositional phrase acts as an adjective telling what kind of 'characteristic', while *in the brain,* describing 'storm', ends the clause. Sentence two begins with a phrasal adverb – *two weeks later* – that modifies the verb 'suffered'. The comma after 'seizure' marks the end of the first independent clause and with the co-ordinating conjunction *and*, the second independent clause begins. Within that clause is the important information contained in the prepositional phrase *on anti-convulsive medication.*

Do you recognise the first word of sentence three and its part of speech? *By her fourth birthday* begins with a preposition and the phrase functions as an adverb telling when. Sentence four varies the construction by having the independent clause first, followed by a phrasal adverb, *suddenly affecting only the right side of her body.* This phrase tells how the seizures changed and it ends with an adjective prepositional phrase *of her body* that describes 'side'.

Carrying on to sentence five we can spot a punctuation clue in the semicolon after 'consciousness' that divides the two independent clauses. The compound participial phrases with prepositional phrases are joined by the co-ordinating conjunction *and*. *Which* words are the participles in those phrases, words that look like verbs, but are used as adjectives to modify 'seizures'? They're the adjective *-ing* words, 'originating' and 'disrupting'. Participles are something we haven't seen before in this excerpt. Look at sentence six to find something else. In the middle of the sentence is the infinitive phrase *to talk normally,* describing what Maranda is unable to do. It acts as an adverb stating how the seizures affect her.

Every sentence of Carson's explanation contains phrases, clauses and usually a connecting word or two, making it possible to dissect this excerpt as thoroughly as a doctor might examine a brain! Sentence eight adds variety in beginning with an adverb (*only*), followed by a prepositional phrase (*during sleep*) also used as an adverb, as well as in reversing the order of the subject (*she*) and verb (*was*). Putting the verb first usually happens in an interrogative sentence (when the writer is asking a question) but here the reversed word order points to something the author feels is most important: the hyphenated phrasal adjective, *seizure-free*.

Dependent clauses outnumber independent ones in sentence 10 as the only words that can stand alone are the first two, 'We know'. Have a closer look at the dependent clause beginning with *that*. It is a clause so it needs a subject and a verb: *halves* (subject) and *are* (verb 'aren't' includes the adverb 'not').

NUMBERING AND DEFINITION OF THE ORGANS.

1. AMATIVENESS, Love between the sexes.
A. CONJUGALITY, Matrimony—love of one. [etc.
2. PARENTAL LOVE, Regard for offspring, pets,
3. FRIENDSHIP, Adhesiveness—sociability.
4. INHABITIVENESS, Love of home
5. CONTINUITY, One thing at a time.
E. VITATIVENESS, Love of life.
6. COMBATIVENESS, Resistance—defense.
7. DESTRUCTIVENESS, Executiveness—force.
8. ALIMENTIVENESS, Appetite—hunger.
9. ACQUISITIVENESS, Accumulation.
10. SECRETIVENESS, Policy—management.
11. CAUTIOUSNESS, Prudence—provision.
12. APPROBATIVENESS, Ambition—display.
13. SELF-ESTEEM, Self-respect—dignity.
14. FIRMNESS, Decision—perseverance.
15. CONSCIENTIOUSNESS, Justice, equity.
16. HOPE, Expectation—enterprise.
17. SPIRITUALITY, Intuition—faith—credulity.
18. VENERATION, Devotion—respect.
19. BENEVOLENCE, Kindness—goodness.

20. CONSTRUCTIVENESS, Mechanical ingenuity
21. IDEALITY, Refinement—taste—purity.
B. SUBLIMITY, Love of grandeur—infinitude.
22. IMITATION, Copying—patterning.
23. MIRTHFULNESS, Jocoseness—wit—fun.
24. INDIVIDUALITY, Observation.
25. FORM, Recollection of shape.
26. SIZE, Measuring by the eye.
27. WEIGHT, Balancing—climbing.
28. COLOR, Judgment of colors.
29. ORDER, Method—system—arrangement
30. CALCULATION, Mental arithmetic.
31. LOCALITY, Recollection of places.
32. EVENTUALITY, Memory of facts.
33. TIME, Cognizance of duration.
34. TUNE, Sense of harmony and melody.
35. LANGUAGE, Expression of ideas.
36. CAUSALITY, Applying causes to effect. [tion.
37. COMPARISON, Inductive reasoning—illustra-
C. HUMAN NATURE, Perception of motives.
D. AGREEABLENESS, Pleasantness—suavity.

NOW THAT I'VE FINISHED, WHAT DID I

In between them is the prepositional phrase *of* **the brain,** used as an adjective relating to 'halves'. And following the verb is another dependent clause that we recognise by the *as* clues. Removing our *that* clause and ***as rigidly divided as we once thought*** (including its phrasal adjective) leaves the first two words of the sentence standing all alone. Every other word of the sentence supports the main clause in saying what 'we' do 'know'.

Sentence 12 begins with the co-ordinating conjunction *but* as it closely follows the thought of brain functions mentioned in sentence 11. A conjunction is used as the first word of both sentences but the difference between those conjunctions is important to note. 'Although' can't begin a clause that can stand alone, 'but' can – and does.

Can you identify all six prepositions in sentence 13? (Don't be confused by the phrasal verb *taken over*. In this case, 'over' is not a preposition – the idiom refers to the new functions a certain 'set of cells' will have.) Finding the prepositions makes it even easier to locate the objects of those short phrases: plasticity, set, cells, brain, set, cells. While we may not understand all the concepts surrounding brain surgery, we can comprehend the grammar behind Carson's description by using our brains and concentrating!

What benefit can a writer derive from such a dissection of literature? For a start, looking closely at what others have written gives us ideas for our own writing – the more we read, the more we learn about how others write; the more we learn about others' word choices, the easier it

WRITE THAT WAS REALLY WORTH SAYING?

is for us to try them out for ourselves. However, it's one thing to study a writing style and just try to mimic it; it's an entirely different task to fill a blank page with correct grammar and expression of our own. Think about it this way: other writers can be our support team. We can study their techniques and, by doing so, try to make what we say more effective. When we understand the process of using appropriate words, phrases, clauses and conjunctions to write good sentences, we can concentrate on our ideas instead of each specific word.

What have we learnt in this book that may help our writing? Let's look at the lengthy list: prepositional phrases; verbal phrases – gerunds, participles and infinitives; participial prepositions; verb phrases; phrasal adjectives and adverbs; phrasal verbs; transitions; independent and dependent clauses (including relative clauses); elliptical constructions and co-ordinating, subordinating, correlative and adverb conjunctions. Although learning all of these names and functions may seem daunting at first, understanding these pieces of grammar helps us evaluate our writing to make it better. Consider motivational speaker Coleman Cox's question, 'Now that it's over, what did you really do yesterday that's worth mentioning?' Transfer that thought to how you view your completed writing projects, even the smallest parts, by asking yourself: 'Now that I've finished, what did I write that was really worth saying?' Putting phrases, clauses and conjunctions together correctly, we can make meaningful sentences. And that's why we write!

BUILD YOUR OWN SENTENCE
Match point

The examples opposite from *O Pioneers!* (1913) give American novelist Willa Cather's (1873–1947) description of the harsh frontier in the US state of Nebraska. Number your paper from 1 to 10 and correctly match the grammar elements in column A with the examples from column B. While some answers may appear to have more than one correct choice, there is only one best answer for each.

COLUMN **A**	COLUMN **B**
1. co-ordinating conjunction	A. Although it was only four o'clock
2. subordinating conjunction	B. The light fell upon the two sad young faces
3. infinitive phrase	C. that were turned mutely towards it
4. prepositional phrase	D. who seemed to be looking with such anguished perplexity
5. relative pronoun	E. The homesteads were few and far apart
6. sentence fragment	F. here and there a windmill gaunt against the sky
7. conjunctive adverb	G. seemed to overwhelm the little beginnings
8. independent clause	H. as if it had never been
9. dependent 'that' clause	I. a sod house crouching in a hollow
10. participial phrase	J. But the great fact was the land itself

ANSWER KEY

1.J, 2.H, 3.G, 4.B, 5.D, 6.F, 7.A, 8.E, 9.C, 10.I

GLOSSARY

compound objects: two or more persons or things to which a specified action is directed

compound sentence: a sentence that has two or more independent clauses that are often joined by a comma and a conjunction

compound subject: two or more subjects using the same verb in a sentence

correlate: to have a comparable, shared relationship, as with two correlative conjunctions that are used together (*either* and *or*)

fragment: a group of words that is capitalised and punctuated as a sentence, but is an incomplete thought

helping verb: a verb that provides additional help to the main verb (*am, is, are, was, has, have, had,* etc.)

idiom: a group of words that has a different meaning from the definitions of the individual words

inaugural address: a speech made by a US president marking the beginning of the term of office

literally: using the individual definitions of words to mean exactly what you are saying

main clause: a group of words with a subject and a verb that makes sense by itself and to which other dependent clauses may be connected

object: a person or thing to which a specified action is directed

objective case: the classification of nouns and pronouns that function as receivers of action or as objects of prepositions (*me, us, you, him, her, it, them*)

part of speech: the class or category into which a word may be grouped according to its form changes and its grammatical function; in English, the main parts of speech are verbs, nouns, pronouns, adjectives, adverbs, prepositions, conjunctions and interjections

participial prepositional phrase: a participle of a verb (such as an *-ing* or *-ed* verb form) that begins a prepositional phrase, a group of words consisting of a preposition, its object and any modifiers

predicate: the part of a clause or sentence containing a verb and stating something about the subject

punctuation: marks used to provide meaning and separate elements within sentences, such as full stops, commas, question marks, exclamation marks, semicolons, colons, hyphens and brackets (parentheses)

sentence: a unit of expression that contains a subject and a verb, and expresses a complete, independent thought

subordinate: to be dependent upon something else; to link a group of words with a subject and verb that cannot stand alone to an independent clause that can

tense: the property of the verb that designates time as present, past, future or perfect using single-word verbs and auxiliaries (or helping verbs)

RESOURCES

Eats, Shoots & Leaves: The Zero Tolerance Approach to Punctuation by Lynne Truss, Profile Books/Fourth Estate, 2003/2009

My Grammar and I (or should that be 'Me'?): Old-School Ways to Sharpen your English by Caroline Taggart and J A Wines, Michael O'Mara Books, 2008

New Hart's Rules: the Handbook of Style for Writers and Editors adapted by R M Ritter from Horace Hart's original book, Oxford University Press, 2005

Oxford A-Z of Grammar and Punctuation by John Seely, Oxford University Press, 2009

Oxford English Thesaurus for Schools by Susan Rennie and John Mannion, Oxford University Press, 2010

For online punctuation lessons, go to: *www.grammar-monster.com/*

This BBC website has several games for learning punctuation: *www.bbc.co.uk/ schools/ks2bitesize/english/spelling_grammar/*

INDEX